W9-CGS-023

Mega-Fun

Card-Game Math

by Karol L. Yeatts

SCHOLASTIC
PROFESSIONAL BOOKS

New York • Toronto • London • Auckland • Sydney
Mexico City • New Delhi • Hong Kong

To Jim (my king) and
Bonnie, Cindi, and Daryl
(my royal friends)

Teachers may photocopy the reproducible pages in this book for classroom use. No other part of this publication
may be reproduced in whole or in part, or stored in a retrieval system, or transmitted in any form or by any means,
electronic, mechanical, photocopying, recording, or otherwise, without written permission of the publisher.
For information regarding permission, write to Scholastic Inc., 555 Broadway, New York, NY 10012.

Cover design by Norma Ortiz
Cover and interior illustrations by Rick Brown, except pages 42–47 by Delana Bettoli
Interior design by Sydney Wright
ISBN: 0-439-04090-6
Copyright © 2000 by Karol L. Yeatts
All rights reserved. Printed in the U.S.A.

Contents

Introduction

Welcome to *Mega-Fun Card-Game Math*! These 25 easy-to-play card games and activities will help your students "ace" math by reinforcing all the essential skills. With a partner or in a small group, kids will have fun as they practice using place value, recognizing even and odd numbers, adding, subtracting, multiplying, and more—all with just a deck of playing cards!

Cards offer a fun and natural link to math concepts. Even the most simple card games help children develop number recognition. The different attributes of cards provide wonderful opportunities for classifying and sorting. Kids explore attributes such as color, suit, even and odd numbers, and more as they create patterns and use Venn diagrams. Many of the games reinforce addition and subtraction, helping kids gain speed as they play again and again. You'll even find games and activities that involve measurement, probability, problem solving, and basic logical reasoning.

All of the games and activities in this book correspond to the standards recommended by the National Council of Teachers of Mathematics (NCTM). Refer to the chart on page 6 to find out how each activity connects to the NCTM Standards 2000. The activities in this book are arranged in order of complexity. For each math concept or operation, there are several games at varying levels of difficulty. This will help you meet the needs of all of your students from the first week of the school year to the last! Many of the games offer variations so that you can adapt them as you see fit. Read through the section titled How to Use This Book on page 5 for specific suggestions about using the games in your classroom. In the back of the book, you'll find a reproducible deck of cards so that you can make and replace cards as needed.

These games and activities are easy to play and require little to no preparation. Once you show kids the rules, they'll be ready to play on their own anytime—at lunch, before school, when they have completed other work, and even at home with family members. Get ready to deal out some fun-tastic math learning!

How to Use This Book

The games and activities in this book correlate to the NCTM Standards 2000. Use the skills chart on page 6 to find games that reinforce a particular standard. The games are arranged in order of difficulty, beginning with number recognition, counting, and place-value activities and moving through addition, subtraction, multiplication, measurement, probability, and more. The skills covered in each game are listed at the top of each page, followed by step-by-step directions. Some games include a reproducible game sheet as well.

After you have introduced a particular skill, choose an easy game that reinforces that skill. First, show students how to play the game. Then observe them playing to make sure they understand the rules and to assess their skill level for a particular concept or operation. As children's skills develop, introduce new and more challenging games.

In the back of the book, you'll find a deck of reproducible playing cards. It is best to photocopy these on sturdy paper and laminate them for greater durability. You may wish to have students color the diamonds and hearts red. (The spades and clubs are already colored black.)

Properties of Cards

There are 52 cards in a deck and four suits: hearts, diamonds, clubs, and spades. Explain to children what constitutes a full deck of cards. Also discuss the importance of shuffling cards before they begin a game. Most of the games in this book call for a deck of cards with the face cards removed (jack, queen, king). The ace is used to represent the number 1. The face cards are used in games that involve sorting, classifying, patterning, and probability. For some activities, you can use mismatched or incomplete decks of cards. This is noted in the materials section of these games. Save any incomplete decks for these games and activities.

Before Beginning

Designate a corner or other space in the classroom for playing cards. Since children are often more comfortable on the floor, it is a good idea to use a special rug for the game area. Show kids where cards are stored and how to put them away. Explain the importance of keeping cards in the same place so that they don't get lost. You may wish to store the reproducible game sheets and pencils in the game area as well.

Before introducing the games, it is helpful to talk about what it means to be a good sport. It is also a good idea to remind students that the point of playing the games is to have fun, to spend time with classmates, and to sharpen their skills.

Who Goes First?

Choosing who goes first in a game can be decided in several different ways. Brainstorm with children ways to determine playing order. Here are some suggestions:

♠ Each player draws a card. The player with the greater-value card goes first.

♦ Each player draws a card. The player with the lower-value card goes first.

♥ Each player draws two cards and adds their value. The player with the greater sum goes first.

♣ Each player draws two cards and adds their value. The player with the lower sum goes first.

♠ Each player says a number from 1 to 10. The top card is drawn from the deck. The player whose number is closest to the card goes first.

Connection With the NCTM Standards 2000

Activity	Number and Operations	Estimation*	Number Sense and Numeration*	Concepts of Whole-Number Operations*	Whole-Number Computation*	Fractions*	Algebra	Geometry	Measurement	Data Analysis and Probability	Problem Solving	Reasoning and Proof	Communication	Connections	Representation
What's Next?	●		●	●	●										
Odds and Evens	●		●									●		●	●
Find Your Place Value	●		●								●			●	●
Guess My Card	●		●								●	●	●		
Card Sort	●		●				●				●	●	●	●	●
Card Patterns	●		●				●					●	●	●	●
Add a Pair	●		●	●	●		●							●	●
A Game, More or Less	●		●	●	●							●			
1 More or 1 Less	●		●	●	●							●		●	●
Take 10!	●		●	●	●							●			●
Solitary 11	●		●	●	●							●			
"Oh, No!"	●		●	●	●					●					
Even and Odd Sums	●		●	●	●		●					●	●	●	●
Adding On	●		●	●	●										
Multiply, Multiply	●		●	●	●									●	●
Card Builders								●				●	●	●	●
Measure Three Ways	●	●	●	●	●	●		●	●			●	●	●	●
A Family of Cards	●		●	●	●		●					●			●
Card Combos	●		●	●	●						●	●			
Card Facts	●		●	●	●							●		●	●
Go for 10!	●		●	●	●							●		●	●
Calculating Cards	●		●	●	●							●		●	●
Card Challenge	●		●	●	●							●		●	●
Balancing Act	●		●	●	●		●					●			
What's the Chance?	●		●								●	●	●	●	●
Card Teasers	●		●								●	●	●	●	●

* Indicates a subcategory of Number and Operations

Players: 2

This game reinforces visual memory, number recognition, and number order as children collect a sequence from 1 to 10.

Materials

20 cards of any suit (2 each of the numbers 1–10. Ace = 1)

The Way to Play

1 One player shuffles the cards and places them facedown in four rows (five cards per row).

2 The object is to be the first player to collect ten cards of any suit in order from 1 (ace) to 10.

3 Player 1 chooses any card and turns it over.

♠ If the card is not a 1, the player turns the card back over and the turn ends.

♦ If the card is a 1, the player keeps it and chooses another card.

♥ If the second card is not a 2, the player turns the card back over and the turn ends.

♣ If the second card is a 2, the player keeps it and chooses another card.

A player continues to choose cards as long as the numbers are drawn in sequential order.

4 Player 2 takes a turn in the same way as Player 1, building his or her own sequence starting with 1.

5 Players continue to take turns. On each turn, a player continues to build the sequence from where he or she left off on the last turn.

6 The first player to collect the cards 1–10 in sequential order wins.

♠ **Variation** ♣

Challenge children to play "Blast Off" by collecting cards in reverse order from 10 to 1.

Odds and Evens

This guessing game reinforces the concepts of even and odd numbers and involves chance.

Materials

♦ ♦ ♦ ♦ ♦ ♦ ♦ ♦ ♦

1 shuffled deck of cards with face cards removed

The Way to Play

♦ ♦ ♦ ♦ ♦ ♦ ♦ ♦ ♦ ♦ ♦ ♦ ♦ ♦

1) Stack the cards facedown in a pile.

2) To take a turn, a player guesses whether the top card in the pile is odd or even and then turns it face-up. If the guess is correct, the player keeps the card and takes another turn. If the guess is incorrect, the player places the card in a discard pile. A player continues to turn over cards until a guess is incorrect.

3) Players take turns until there are no more cards in the pile.

4) The player with the most cards wins.

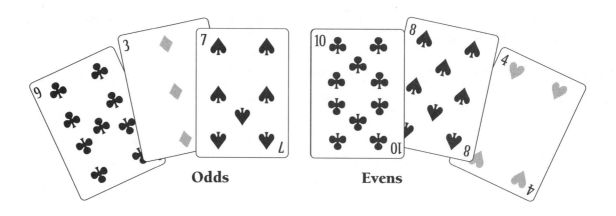

Odds   **Evens**

Find Your Place Value

Players: 2–4

Children review place value as they create the greatest three-digit numbers using cards.

Materials

1 shuffled deck of cards with tens and face cards removed
(**NOTE:** If there are more than two players, you may wish to use two decks of cards with tens and face cards removed.)

The Way to Play

1 One player deals the cards evenly among the players.

2 Players place their cards in a stack facedown in front of them.

3 Each player turns over three cards. Each player arranges his or her cards to make the greatest possible three-digit number.

4 Each player reads his or her number aloud. The player with the greatest number wins all of the cards from that round and places them in a separate pile.

5 Play continues until all cards have been used.

6 The player with the most cards at the end of the game wins.

hundreds	tens	ones
9 ♥	3 ♠	A ♣

♠ Variation ♣

Players can use four or more cards to work with greater place values.
Children can also form the lowest possible number to win each round.

Players: 2–4

Children review concepts of greater than and less than as they guess the secret number card.

Materials

1 shuffled deck of cards with face cards removed
pencils

The Way to Play

1 Stack the cards facedown in a pile.

2 One player selects any card from the pile without showing it to the other players.

3 The other players take turns guessing the number on the "secret card."

4 After a guess is made, the player holding the card responds by saying either, "It's greater than that number" or "It's less than that number."

5 If the number is not guessed correctly after each player has had two chances to guess, the player holding the card keeps the card. That player then chooses another card and another round of guessing begins. If a player correctly guesses the number, that player keeps the card and then chooses the next secret card.

6 The game continues until one player has three cards.

For example:

Molly chooses a card with the number 4.
Dario guesses 3.
Molly says, "It's greater than 3."
Shira guesses 5.
Molly says, "It's less than 5."
Dario guesses the correct number, 4.
Molly gives the secret card to Dario.
Dario chooses a card and the other players guess what it is. The game ends when one player has collected three cards.

♠ Variation ♣

For more of a challenge, children can try to guess the exact card
(for example, a three of hearts) rather than just the number. Children can ask
questions such as, "Is it a red suit?" Is it a heart? Is it an odd number?"

Card Sort

Children use Venn diagrams to
sort and classify cards by attributes.

Materials (for each group of 3–4 students)

1 shuffled deck of cards
2 four-foot lengths of string

The Way to Play

1 Arrange a string in the shape of a circle on the floor and have students gather around. Think of a rule to determine which cards are placed inside the circle and which are placed outside; for example, even-numbered cards are placed inside and odd-numbered cards are placed outside. Place a few cards according to the rule and ask children to guess the rule. Challenge children to think of different rules and place the cards accordingly.

2 Make a Venn diagram by arranging two overlapping circles on the floor. Think of a rule for placing the cards in the circles; for example, one circle is for red cards and the other is for odd-numbered cards. The overlapping section is for cards that are both red and odd-numbered. (**NOTE:** If a card does not belong in the Venn diagram, it is placed outside the two circles. In this example, black, even-numbered cards are placed outside the circle.)

3 Have children choose a card and place it in the correct part of the Venn diagram. As they do this, have them give the reason for placing the card in that section. Ask children to think of other rules to sort the cards.

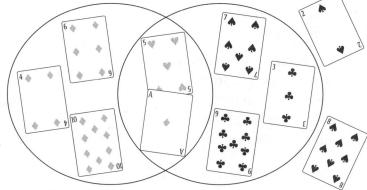

4 Give each group two pieces of string to form a Venn diagram. One player in each group thinks of a rule without revealing it. Each of the other players takes a turn placing a card. The player who made up the rule says if a card is placed according to the rule. If a player has placed a card correctly, he or she can guess the rule. A player who guesses a rule correctly earns a point. Then the next player takes a turn by making up a new rule, and play continues in the same way.

5 The game ends when each player has thought of a rule. The player with the most points wins.

Card Patterns

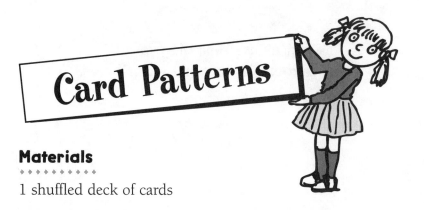

Players: 2

Children create patterns using the various attributes of cards.

Materials

1 shuffled deck of cards

The Way to Play

1 One player deals the cards evenly between the two players.

2 Player 1 creates a pattern using any six cards from his or her hand. The pattern can be based on color, suit, number, odd vs. even numbers, face vs. number card, and so on.

(**NOTE:** Students should choose a two- or three-unit pattern so it repeats within six cards. This provides the other player with sufficient information to determine the pattern. Younger children may want to use only one attribute in the pattern, such as suit.)

Older students may want to incorporate more than one attribute in the pattern, such as suit and even and odd numbers.

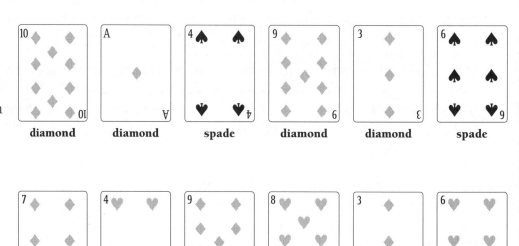

| diamond | diamond | spade | diamond | diamond | spade |

| odd diamond | even heart | odd diamond | even heart | odd diamond | even heart |

3 Player 2 reads the pattern aloud. For example, the player would say, "The pattern is diamond, diamond, spade, diamond, diamond, spade." (If he or she cannot find the pattern, Player 1 reads the pattern.)

4 Player 2 tries to add three of his or her cards to the pattern. If successful, Player 2 earns a point and the turn ends. If unsuccessful, the player earns no points and the turn ends. At the end of the turn, players keep their own cards.

5 Players take turns until one player has reached ten points.

Add a Pair

This variation of Concentration reinforces number recognition and visual memory as children practice adding doubles.

Materials

1 shuffled deck of cards with face cards removed
pencils
Add a Pair Game Sheet, one per player
    (page 14, optional)
calculator (optional)

The Way to Play

1 Each player takes a game sheet and a pencil.

2 Players arrange the cards facedown in five rows.

3 To take a turn, a player chooses two cards and turns them over. If the cards do not match, the player turns them back over and the turn ends. If the cards match, the player adds the numbers on the cards and records the addition problem on the game sheet (page 14) or another sheet of paper. The player keeps the cards and takes another turn.

4 Players take turns until all cards have been matched.

5 Each player adds all the sums in the right-hand column of the game sheet and writes the total sum in the box at the bottom of the page. (Players can also use a calculator for this step.) The player with the greatest number wins.

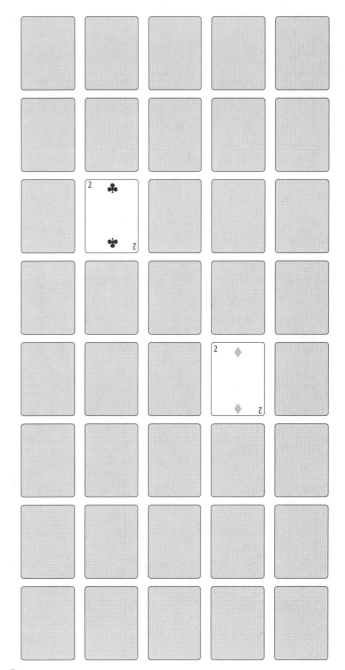

Name _____ Date _____

Add a Pair Game Sheet

Card 1	+	Card 2	=	Sum

Mega-Fun Card-Game Math Scholastic Professional Books

A Game, More or Less

Players: 2

Children compare the values of cards and practice simple addition and subtraction.

Materials

1 shuffled deck of cards with face cards removed

The Way to Play

1 One player deals the cards evenly between the two players. Players stack their cards facedown in front of them.

2 Both players turn over their top card. The first player to take a turn compares the value of the two cards by answering these questions:

♠ Is mine more or less?

♦ How many more? or How many less?

3 The player with the greater-value card wins both cards and puts them in a separate stack. If the cards are equal, players draw again and the winner takes both pairs of cards.
(**NOTE:** Players can decide in advance if they would like the player with the lesser-value card to win the cards instead.)

4 Players continue to take turns until all cards have been played. The player with the most cards wins.

1 More or 1 Less

Players: 2 or more

This variation of Go Fish reinforces adding and subtracting 1.

Materials

1 shuffled deck of cards with face cards removed

The Way to Play

1 One player deals five cards to each player and stacks the remaining cards facedown in a pile.

2 Player 1 chooses a card from his or her hand. Player 1 asks another player for a card that is "1 more or 1 less" than the chosen card. For example, Player 1 chooses a 3 and asks Player 2, "Do you have a card that is 1 more or 1 less than 3?"

3 • If Player 2 has either a 4 or a 2, he or she gives the card to Player 1. (If Player 2 has both a 4 and a 2, he or she chooses which card to give Player 1.) Player 1 places the original card and the card from Player 2 in a separate pile and asks for another card in the same way.

• If Player 2 has neither a 4 nor a 2, Player 1 chooses a card from the deck and the turn ends.

4 A player continues to ask for cards until the other player does not have a requested card. The asking player then chooses a card from the deck and the turn ends.

5 Players continue to take turns. The first player to run out of cards in his or her hand wins.

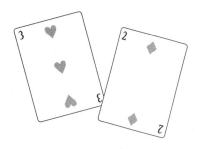 

♠ Variation ♣

Children can play a similar game by asking for cards that are "2 more or 2 less" than the chosen number, "3 more or 3 less," and so on.

Take 10!

Children review addition as they win cards with sums that are greater or less than 10.

Materials

1 shuffled deck of cards with face cards removed

The Way to Play

1 One player stacks the cards facedown in a pile.

2 Players decide who will collect cards that are "less than 10" and who will collect cards that are "10 or more."

3 To take a turn, a player draws two cards. The player adds the number on the cards and says the equation aloud. (For example, a player would say, "9 plus 5 equals 14.")

4 If the sum of the numbers is less than 10, the "less than 10" player wins the cards. If the sum is 10 or more, the "10 or more" player wins the cards.

5 Players take turns until all cards have been played.

6 The player with the most cards wins.

5 + 9 = 14
14 is more than 10

3 + 6 = 9
9 is less than 10

Players: 1

This simple variation of Solitaire involves creating addition problems with sums of 11.

Materials

1 shuffled deck of cards with face cards removed

The Way to Play

1 The player arranges nine cards faceup in three rows of three, and stacks the rest facedown in a pile.

2 From these nine cards, the player picks up two or more cards that have a sum of 11. The player fills the spaces with cards from the pile. (If there are no cards that add up to 11, the player adds another row of three cards from the pile.)

3 The player continues to choose cards whose values add up to 11.

4 The game ends when all of the cards from the pile have been used and no cards remain whose numbers add up to 11.

5 To extend learning, the player counts the number of cards left at the end of the game and writes down that number. The player shuffles the cards thoroughly and plays again. The object is to have fewer cards left at the end of the second game than the first.

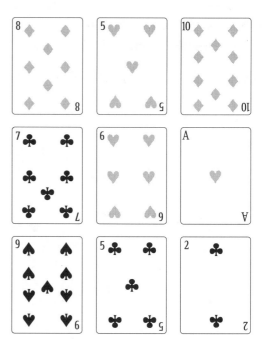

♠ Variation ♣

Children can look for cards whose values add up to other numbers, such as 12, 13, 14, and so on.

"Oh, No!"

Children practice addition and take their chances as they collect cards until an "Oh, no!" card is drawn.

Materials

1 shuffled deck of cards with face cards removed

The Way to Play

1 A player stacks the cards facedown in a pile. At the beginning of each round, a player draws a card. Any card with this number will be an "Oh, no!" card. (For any number drawn, there will be four "Oh, no!" cards.) The card is returned to the deck and the cards are shuffled again.

2 The object of the game is to collect as many cards as possible before an "Oh, no!" card is drawn. Players take turns turning over the top card from the deck. Players keep the cards they turn over. At any time before an "Oh, no!" card is drawn, a player can choose to stop drawing cards. When players choose to stop, they say "Stop!" and place their cards facedown. This signals to other players that they are out of the round. When a player stops, the player adds the values of his or her cards from that round. The sum is recorded as the player's score.

3 When an "Oh, no!" card is drawn, all players who are still drawing cards lose their cards and receive no points for that round. If only one player was drawing cards, only that player loses his or her cards. If all players choose to stop drawing cards before an "Oh, no!" card is drawn, they all add the values of their cards from that round and record their score. Then one player draws a new "Oh, no!" card from the deck and the next round begins.

4 After an "Oh, no!" card is drawn, all cards are returned to the deck and reshuffled. A new "Oh, no!" card is drawn, and play continues in the same way. The game ends when a player reaches or exceeds 50 points.

Even and Odd Sums

Children discover the patterns that result from adding even and odd numbers.

Materials

1 shuffled deck of cards with face cards removed
Even and Odd Sums Game Sheet, one per player (page 21)
pencils

The Way to Play

1 One player stacks the cards facedown in a pile.

2 Each player takes a pencil and a game sheet.

3 Each player takes two cards from the pile and identifies the number on each as either even or odd.

4 Each player adds the numbers on the two cards and says whether the sum is even or odd.

5 On the game sheet, each player records the numbers and whether they are even or odd. Each player records the sum and whether it is even or odd. Cards are placed in a discard pile.

6 Play continues in the same way until all cards have been drawn.

7 Players answer the questions at the bottom of their game sheets by counting the number of even and odd sums. The player with the most even sums wins. (Players can also decide in advance if they would like the winner to have the most odd sums.)

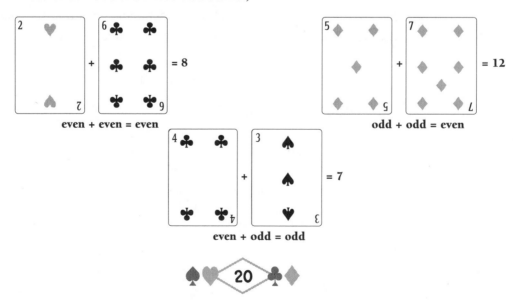

even + even = even

odd + odd = even

even + odd = odd

Name _____ Date _____

Even and Odd Sums Game Sheet

Card 1 +	Card 2 =	Sum
Number (even/odd)	Number (even/odd)	Number (even/odd)
5 (odd)	7 (odd)	12 (even)

How many even sums do you have? _____

How many odd sums do you have? _____

Mega-Fun Card-Game Math Scholastic Professional Books

Players: 2

Children review even and odd numbers as they add on to a growing sum. This game involves regrouping.

Materials

1 shuffled deck of cards with face cards removed
scrap paper
pencils

The Way to Play

1 Players decide who will be "even" and who will be "odd."

2 One player stacks the cards facedown in a pile, turns over the top card, and places it to the right of the pile.

3 To take a turn, Player 1 turns over the top card and places it to the right of the card already turned over. The player adds the values of the two cards.

♠ If the player is "even" and the sum is even, the player earns a point.

♦ If the player is "even" and the sum is odd, the player does not earn a point.

♥ If the player is "odd" and the sum is odd, the player earns a point.

♣ If the player is "odd" and the sum is even, the player does not earn a point.

Player 1 leaves the cards where they are, and the turn ends.

4 Player 2 turns over the top card from the stack and places it to the right of the two cards. The player adds the value of that card to the sum of the first two cards. The player follows the rules listed above to determine if he or she earns a point.

5 Players continue to take turns by adding the value of the next card to the sum of the previous cards.

6 The first player to reach five points wins.

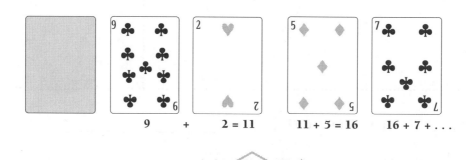

9 + 2 = 11   11 + 5 = 16   16 + 7 + . . .

Multiply, Multiply

Materials

1 shuffled deck of cards with face cards removed

The Way to Play

1 One player deals the cards evenly between the two players.

2 Each player turns over two cards.

3 Each player multiplies the numbers on the two cards. Each player says his or her multiplication problem and answer aloud.

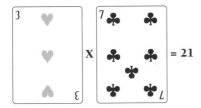
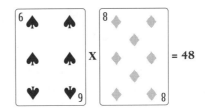

4 If only one player answers correctly, that player wins both pairs of cards. If both players answer correctly, the player with the greater answer wins both pairs. When players win cards, they should stack them in a separate pile.

5 The game continues until all cards have been played. The player with the most cards wins.

♠ Variation ♣

When children have mastered their multiplication facts, they can play a game that reinforces speed. Players follow step 1, above. Then, at the same time, each player turns over a card from his or her pile. Players multiply the numbers on the two cards. The first player to say the correct answer wins the cards. The player with the most cards at the end of a given amount of time wins.

Players: any number

Children develop spatial sense as they build two- and three-dimensional shapes with cards.

Materials

several decks of cards
(**NOTE:** It is best to use old cards from incomplete decks since children will tape cards together.)

The Way to Play

1 Give each child a stack of at least 15 cards.

2 As a group, brainstorm a list of two-dimensional shapes (square, rectangle, triangle, rhombus, pentagon, hexagon, octagon, and so on). On the chalkboard or on chart paper, draw and label each shape.

3 Ask children to spread their cards facedown in front of them on the floor or on a desktop. Invite them to form these two-dimensional shapes using their cards.

4 When they are finished, discuss the results. How many cards did they use to create each of the shapes? Were any shapes easier or more difficult to form? Why? Did anyone try to form a circle? Why was this difficult?

5 Next, discuss and define a three-dimensional or solid shape. Have children brainstorm different solid shapes, such as a cube, pyramid, or rectangular prism. On the chalkboard or on chart paper, draw and label these shapes.

6 Invite children to build some of these shapes using cards and tape.

7 Display students' structures, and ask children to talk about how they built their shapes.

8 To extend this activity, invite kids to build free-form structures with cards. Challenge them to do this without using tape. Allow them to experiment first, and then, if needed, show them that it is easiest to balance cards by arranging them in a T shape. See who can balance the most cards!

Measure Three Ways

Children estimate and explore linear measurement, surface area, and capacity, using cards as nonstandard units of measurement.

Materials

several decks of playing cards
(**NOTE:** It is best to use old cards from incomplete decks since children will tape cards together.)
tape
Measure Three Ways Chart, one per player (page 27)
pencils

The Way to Play

LINEAR MEASUREMENT

1 Give each child three playing cards, tape, a pencil, and a copy of the chart on page 27.

2 Lead a discussion about how and why we use measurement. Define basic terms such as *length* and *width*.

3 Have children tape together three playing cards end to end to create a card ruler.

4 Demonstrate how to measure an object using the card ruler. For example, a book might measure three cards long. Discuss how to handle measurements that are not whole numbers, for example 5½ card lengths.

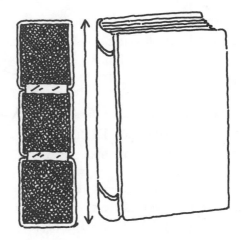

5 Ask children to choose objects from around the classroom to measure in card units. Before they measure, have kids estimate the length of the objects in card units and record their estimates on their charts.

6 Invite children to measure the objects and then record the information on their charts.
(**NOTE:** To turn this into a game, have children figure out whose estimates are closest to the actual measurements.)

Measure Three Ways (Cont.)

SURFACE AREA

1 Discuss and define surface area, using concrete examples such as a desktop or floor mat. Ask children to think about how they could measure surface area.

2 Introduce playing cards as a way to measure surface area. Ask children to think about how to do this. Discuss ways to handle the leftover spaces that are not covered by cards.

3 Challenge children to choose various classroom objects and estimate the surface area of each in card units. Have kids record their estimates on their charts.

4 Invite children to use cards to measure the surface area of the objects. Then have children record the information on their charts.

CAPACITY

1 Discuss and define capacity, using concrete examples such as a shoe box or fish tank. Ask children to think about ways they could determine the capacity of these objects.

2 Show children how to tape together four cards to create a card box, leaving the two ends open. Have each child create several of these.

3 Demonstrate how to use the card boxes to fill a shoe box or other container. Discuss how to handle the leftover empty spaces.

4 Divide the class into groups of 3–4 children. Choose a few rectangular- or square-shaped containers, such as various-sized drawers, boxes, crates, storage bins, and so on. Ask groups to estimate how many card boxes would fill each container. Have kids record their estimates on their charts.

5 Ask children to measure the capacity of the containers by filling them with card boxes. Then have them record their results.

6 Discuss the results. How close were children's estimates to the actual measurements?

Name _____ Date _____

Measure Three Ways Chart

Things I Measured	Estimate	Actual Measurement
LINEAR		
1.		
2.		
3.		
4.		
SURFACE AREA		
1.		
2.		
3.		
4.		
CAPACITY		
1.		
2.		
3.		
4.		

Children build problem-solving skills as they create addition problems with cards.

Materials

1 shuffled deck of cards with face cards removed
scrap paper
pencils

The Way to Play

1 One player deals five cards facedown to each player.

2 At the same time, players turn over their cards. Each player tries to make an addition equation with the largest possible sum. The player can use three or more cards in the equation, including one card as the sum.

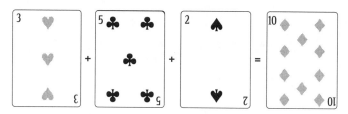

3 If a player makes a correct equation, the player reads the equation aloud. The player records the sum of the equation as his or her points for that round. In the example above, the player earns 10 points.

4 Players return their cards to the stack, and the dealer shuffles the cards.

5 Players repeat steps 1–4. The first player to reach or exceed 50 points wins.

♠ Variation ♣

Children can play a similar game by forming subtraction, multiplication, or division problems.

Card Combos

Children develop problem-solving skills as they create addition and subtraction problems.

Materials

1 shuffled deck of cards with face cards removed
Card Combos Game Sheet, one per player (page 30, optional)
pencils

The Way to Play

1 Each player takes a pencil and a game sheet (or each player can number a sheet of paper from 1 to 15).

2 One player stacks the cards facedown in a pile.

3 The object is to be the first player to cross off all of the numbers on his or her game sheet.

4 To take a turn, a player turns over the top two cards (for example, a 4 and a 5). The player can make either an addition problem or a subtraction problem with the cards ($4 + 5 = 9$ or $5 - 4 = 1$). The player decides which operation to use, and marks off the answer to the problem on the game sheet (for example, 9 or 1). The player places the two cards in a discard pile.
(**NOTE:** A player may not be able to cross off a number on every turn because numbers may already be crossed off.)

5 When all of the cards in the first pile have been used, a player shuffles the cards in the discard pile and those cards are used.

6 Players take turns until one player wins by crossing off all of his or her numbers.

1	6	11
2	7	12
3	8	13
4	9	14
5	10	15

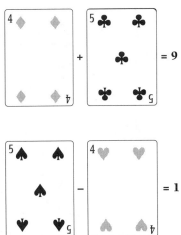

Name _____ Date _____

Card Combos Game Sheet

1	6	11
2	7	12
3	8	13
4	9	14
5	10	15

Mega-Fun Card-Game Math Scholastic Professional Books

Within a set time, children use five cards to create as many addition, subtraction, and multiplication problems as possible.

Materials

1 shuffled deck of cards with face cards removed
paper
pencils
calculator
timer

The Way to Play

1 Each player takes a pencil and a sheet of paper.

2 One player deals five cards to each player and stacks the rest facedown in a pile.

3 One player sets the timer for five minutes and starts it.

4 Each player uses his or her cards to make as many different addition, subtraction, or multiplication problems as possible within the time limit. Only two cards should be used in each problem. Players record both the problem and the solution on a sheet of paper. For example, a player with a 7, 2, 5, 10, and 4 can make these computation problems, among others:

5 When time is up, players check one another's answers. (Calculators can be used.) Players earn one point for each correct answer.

6 The first player to earn 25 points wins. (Players may need to play several rounds. Cards are returned to the deck and shuffled after each round.)

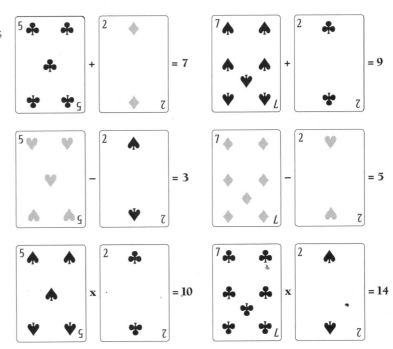

Go for 10!

Within a set time, children create as many addition, subtraction, and multiplication problems as possible that equal 10.

Materials

1 shuffled deck of cards with face cards removed
timer

The Way to Play

1. One player deals ten cards to each player. The player then sets the timer for three minutes and starts it.

2. Players turn their cards over at the same time. During the three minutes, players use their cards to make as many addition, subtraction, or multiplication problems as they can that equal 10. (Each card may be used only once. A 10 card can stand on its own to equal 10.)

3. When time is up, players tell the equations they made. Players keep the cards used in their equations and return the unused cards to the deck.

4. The game continues in the same way until all cards have been used. (The final round will be played with fewer than ten cards per player.)

5. The player with the most cards wins.

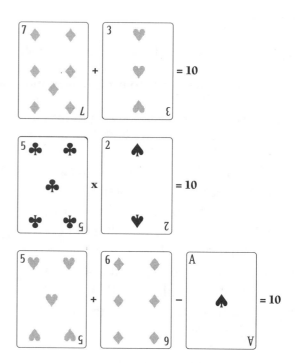

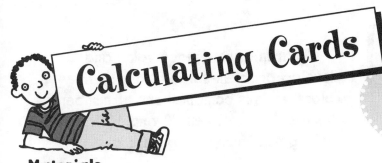

Children review place value and develop problem-solving skills as they form addition and subtraction problems with two-digit numbers. This game involves regrouping.

Materials

1 shuffled deck of cards with tens and face cards removed
paper
pencils
calculator

The Way to Play

1 One player deals four cards to each player and stacks the rest facedown in a pile.

2 The dealer turns over the top two cards and places them side by side.

3 The two cards together form a two-digit "goal number." The first card represents the tens place and the second card represents the ones place. A player reads the goal number aloud.

tens | ones

35

4 Each player arranges his or her four cards to form two 2-digit numbers. The object is to make an addition or subtraction problem whose answer is as close as possible to the goal number. The player with the closest answer scores one point.

For example:

The number drawn from the stack is a 92 (a 9 and a 2). Player 1 arranges her cards to form the numbers 68 and 23. Their sum is 91. Player 2 arranges his cards to form the numbers 57 and 45. Their sum is 102. Since 91 is closer to 92 than 102, Player 1 scores a point.

Player 1
tens | ones

tens | ones

92

Player 1
tens | ones

+

91

+

102

5 Players place the four cards they used from that round in a discard pile.

6 The next round begins by drawing two cards to form a new goal number. Play continues in the same way.

7 The game ends when all cards have been played. The player with the most points wins.

♠ Variation ♣

Children can play a similar game using three- or four-digit numbers.

Card Challenge

Players: 2

Children review place value and develop problem-solving skills as they explore various combinations of numbers whose sum is between 50 and 100. This game involves regrouping.

Materials

2 shuffled decks of cards with tens and face cards removed
calculators (optional)

The Way to Play

1 Player 1 stacks the cards facedown in a pile. Player 1 draws six cards from the deck and, without looking at them, places them facedown beside the pile.

2 Player 1 chooses a "challenge" number between 50 and 100. Player 1 challenges Player 2 to use the six cards to build an addition problem whose sum is as close to the challenge number as possible. (**NOTE:** To form a two-digit number, a player places two cards side by side. The left-hand card represents the tens place and the right-hand card represents the ones place. A player does not have to use all six cards in the problem. Each card may be used only once.)

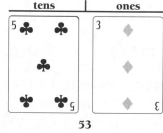

53

3 If Player 2 can form a problem whose sum is within three of the challenge number, Player 2 wins the cards used in the problem. (Children can use calculators to check their work.)

For example: A player is challenged to form an addition problem with a sum of 70. In order to win the cards, the player must form an addition problem whose sum is between 67 and 73. The player uses four cards to form the addition problem 45 + 26. Since the sum of 71 is within three of the challenge number, the player wins all six cards from the round.

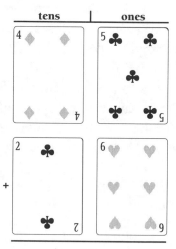

71

4 Players switch roles after each round. The player with the most cards after four rounds wins.

Balancing Act

Players: 2–4

Children balance addition problems with equal sums as a hands-on introduction to the basic algebraic principle of balancing equations.

Materials

1 shuffled deck of cards with face cards removed
Balancing Act Game Sheet, one per player (page 36)

The Way to Play

1 One player deals six cards to each player and stacks the rest of the cards facedown in a pile.

2 Each player chooses four cards from his or her hand to place on the game sheet. The object is to balance the scale by arranging the cards into two addition problems with equal sums. A player earns one point for balancing the scale. For example, a player could place a 7 and a 1 on one side of the scale and a 3 and a 5 on the other (7 + 1 = 3 + 5). A player can also place two cards of the same value on the scale to balance it (4 + 0 = 4 + 0). The player can leave the spaces empty to represent 0.

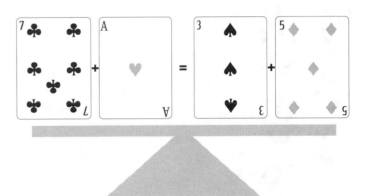

3 At the end of a round, the cards played are placed at the bottom of the deck. The dealer shuffles the cards and gives six more to each player. Play continues in the same way.

4 The game ends when one player reaches ten points (or another predetermined amount).

♠ Variation ♣

Children can play a similar game using addition, subtraction, multiplication, division, or any combination of operations (for example, 2 x 4 = 9 - 1). Make a game sheet similar to the one on page 36, with blank spaces instead of addition symbols. Cut out small squares of paper and write an operation sign on each (+, −, x, ÷). You will need several of each sign. Children can use the operation signs and playing cards to create various balancing equations.

Name _____

Date _____

Balancing Act Game Sheet

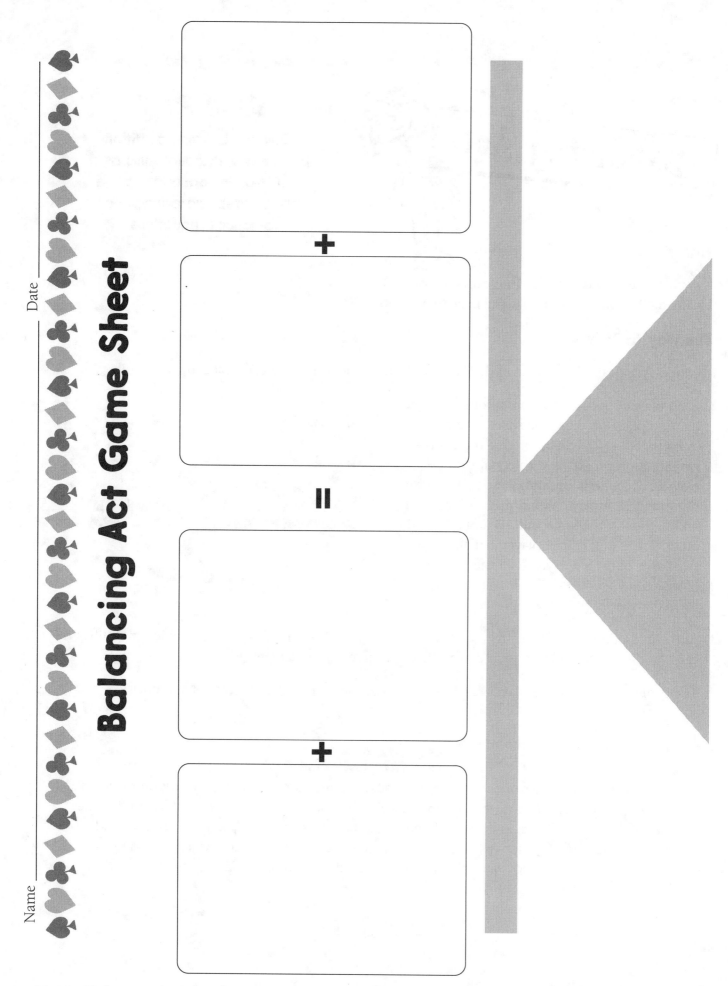

+

=

+

What's the Chance?

Players: any number

Children explore the probability of choosing a card with a particular attribute.

NOTE: This game is designed for older students.

Materials

1 deck of cards for every 3–4 students
"What's the Chance?" Data Sheet, one per player (page 39)
pencils

The Way to Play

1 Explain to children that there are 52 cards in a deck: 26 red cards and 26 black cards. Choose a card from the deck and ask them to guess if it is red or black. Turn it over to show them. Repeat this step a few times.

2 Ask children if they think there is a greater chance of choosing a red card or a black card. Encourage them to explain their responses. Lead them to the conclusion that there is an equal chance because there is an equal number of red and black cards in the deck.

3 Explain that there are 12 face cards (jack, queen, king) in a deck and 40 number cards. Choose a card and have them guess if it is a face card or a number card. Show the card and repeat a few times. Discuss the chances of choosing a face card. Explain that there is a much greater chance of choosing a number card because there are more of them in the deck.

4 If desired, repeat the above steps with other card attributes such as even and odd numbers, cards of different suits, and so on.

5 Divide the class into groups of 3–4 students and give each group a deck of cards. Give each child a pencil and a copy of the data sheet on page 39.

6 Have each group choose two kinds of cards to compare: red vs. black, number vs. face card, even vs. odd number, and so on. Show them where to write this information on the data sheet.

7 Ask kids to figure out how many of each kind of card are in a deck (for example, red vs. black). Based on this information, children can form a hypothesis. What do they think the chances of choosing this type of card are? Show them how to check a box to show their hypothesis.

What's the Chance? (Cont.)

8 Remind kids to shuffle the cards thoroughly before they gather data. Discuss why this is necessary. How might the cards be arranged if someone had sorted them earlier? What does shuffling ensure?

9 Have each group choose one card at a time and record the type of card on the line. They should only record the most relevant information. If they are determining the chances of choosing a red card vs. a black card, they should only record "red" or "black."

10 When they are finished collecting data, children should count how many of each type they chose (such as red or black). Which did they choose more often? How do they interpret these results? Are the chances of choosing one type of card more likely, less likely, or equal to the chances of choosing another type of card?

11 Invite each group to share their findings.

Name _Melinda_   Date _May 3_

"What's the Chance?" Data Sheet

My group is testing the chances of choosing _a number card_ vs.
a face card

Hypothesis: I think that the chances of choosing a _number card_ are (check one):
- ☑ more likely than
- ☐ less likely than
- ☐ the same as
  - choosing a _face card_

Data Collected
(Don't forget to shuffle the cards thoroughly before you begin.)

Pick 1 _number_
Pick 2 _number_
Pick 3 _number_
Pick 4 _face_
Pick 5 _number_
Pick 6 _face_
Pick 7 _number_
Pick 8 _number_
Pick 9 _number_
Pick 10 _face_

What kind of cards did you pick more often? _number_

Conclusion: The data shows that the chances of choosing a _number_ are (check one):
- ☑ more likely than
- ☐ less likely than
- ☐ the same as
  - choosing a _face card_

Name _____ Date _____

"What's the Chance?" Data Sheet

My group is testing the chances of choosing a _____ vs.

a _____ .

Hypothesis: I think that the chances of choosing a _____ are (check one):

☐ more likely than

☐ less likely than

☐ the same as

  choosing a _____ .

Data Collected
(Don't forget to shuffle the cards thoroughly before you begin.)

Pick 1 _____

Pick 2 _____

Pick 3 _____

Pick 4 _____

Pick 5 _____

Pick 6 _____

Pick 7 _____

Pick 8 _____

Pick 9 _____

Pick 10 _____

What kind of cards did you pick more often? _____

Conclusion: The data shows that the chances of choosing a _____ are (check one):

☐ more likely than

☐ less likely than

☐ the same as

  choosing a _____ .

Mega-Fun Card-Game Math Scholastic Professional Books

Card Teasers

Players: any number

Children use problem-solving strategies and logical reasoning to solve a card placement mystery.

NOTE: This game is designed for older students.

Materials

Card Teasers Game Sheet, one per player (page 41)
pencils
reproducible cards, one set per player (below, optional)

The Way to Play

1 Give each player a pencil and a Card Teasers game sheet. You may wish to reproduce the cards below for each child. Children can cut them out and they use them as manipulatives for this activity.

2 Explain to children that five cards have been placed in a row: 5 of spades, 9 of hearts, 6 of hearts, 2 of clubs, and 7 of clubs. (You can place five cards facedown in a row to help them visualize the problem.) Explain that children will use clues to determine the order of five cards from left to right. The five places are numbered 1 to 5.

3 Read the clues together with the children. Show children how to mark an X in each box when they have eliminated a card from a particular position. Explain that kids should draw a smiley face in a box when the clues reveal the correct position for a particular card. Lead children to use a process of elimination to work through the problem.

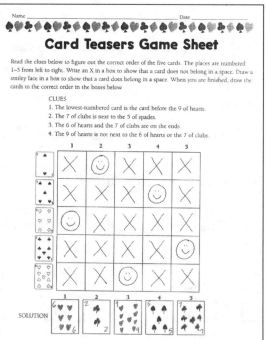

Solution

Card Teasers Game Sheet

Read the clues below to figure out the correct order of the five cards. The places are numbered 1 to 5 from left to right. Write an X in a box to show that a card does not belong in a space. Draw a smiley face in a box to show that a card does belong in a space. When you are finished, draw the cards in the correct order in the boxes below.

CLUES

1. The lowest-numbered card is the card before the 9 of hearts.
2. The 7 of clubs is next to the 5 of spades.
3. The 6 of hearts and the 7 of clubs are on the ends.
4. The 9 of hearts is not next to the 6 of hearts or the 7 of clubs.

	1	2	3	4	5
2♣					
5♠					
6♥					
7♣					
9♥					

SOLUTION

1	2	3	4	5

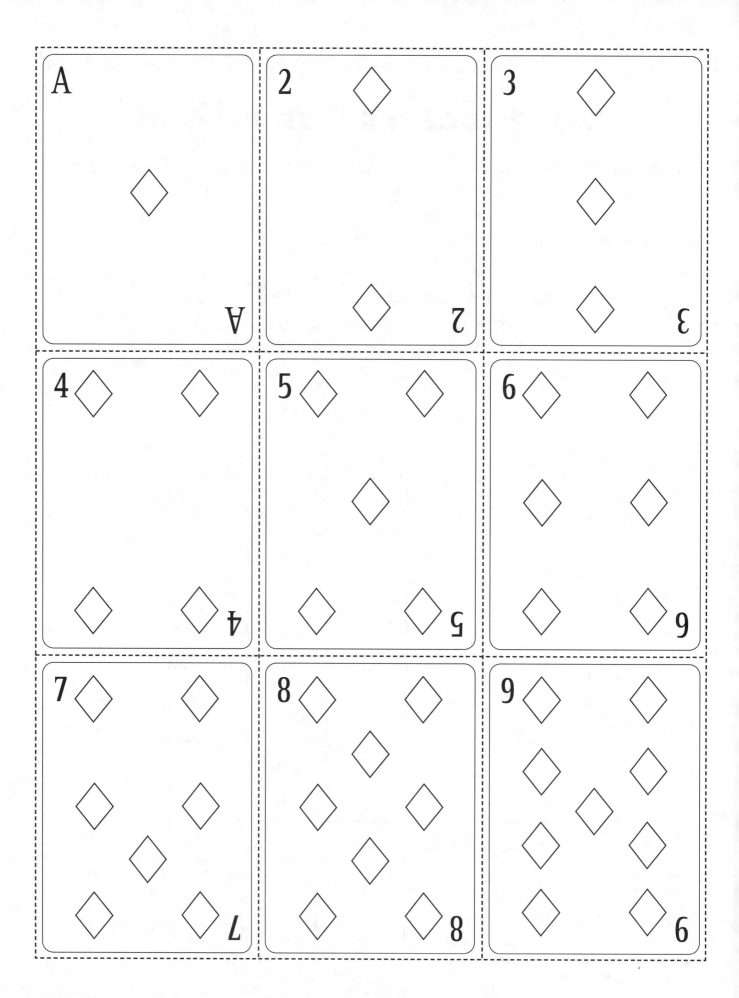

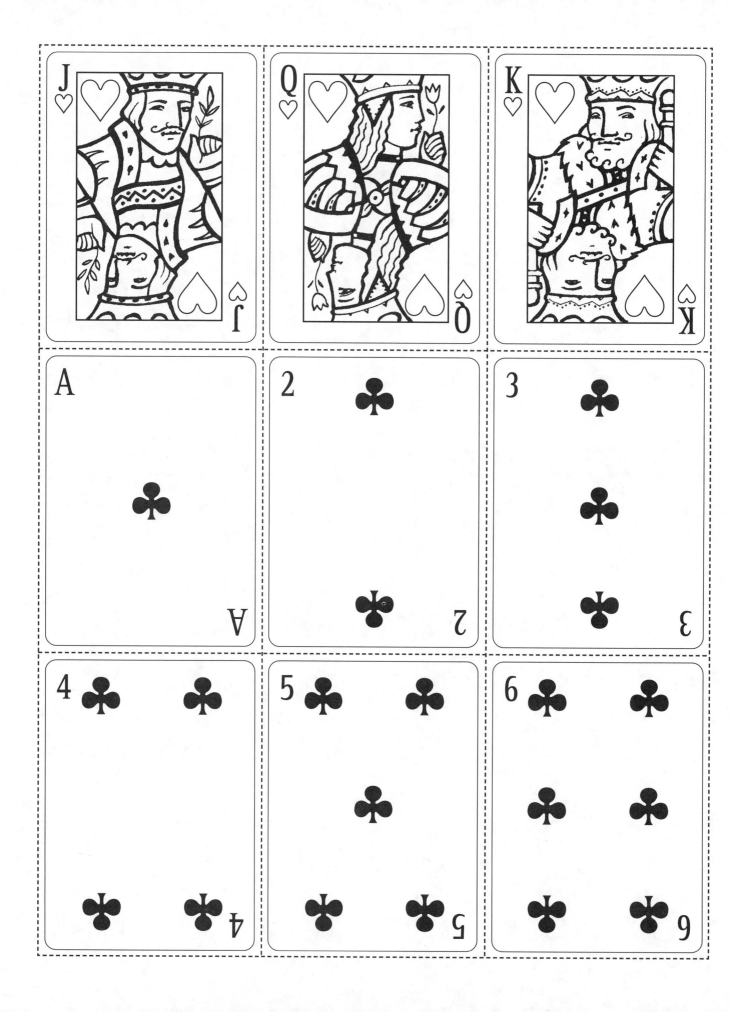

Notes